2 Blessed 2 Be Stressed

2 Blessed 2 Be Stressed

A spiritual guide for a spiritual journey

by Lesia R. Lankford

XULON PRESS

Xulon Press
2301 Lucien Way #415
Maitland, FL 32751
407.339.4217
www.xulonpress.com

© 2020 by Lesia R Lankford

All rights reserved solely by the author. The author guarantees all contents are original and do not infringe upon the legal rights of any other person or work. No part of this book may be reproduced in any form without the permission of the author. The views expressed in this book are not necessarily those of the publisher.

Unless otherwise indicated, Scripture quotations taken from the King James Version (KJV)–*public domain.*

Printed in the United States of America.

ISBN-13: 978-1-6312-9327-6

Table of Contents

Chapter Descriptions ix

Acknowledgments xi

Chapter 1...1

Chapter 2...3

Chapter 3...5

Chapter 4...9

Chapter 5... 11

Chapter 6... 15

Chapter 7... 19

Chapter 8... 21

Chapter 9–Smile 23

Chapter Descriptions

Chapter 1 Description:
"Mmmmm Mmmmm My God"
(In the beginning, it symbolizes unity–First is the kingdom of God.)

Chapter 2 Description:
"Peace, Be Still"
(Two symbolizes being in agreement; "When two or more agree, it shall be done.")

Chapter 3 Description:
"Well Done!"
(Three symbolizes the Trinity: the Father, Son, and the Holy Ghost. Amen!"
"I shall have no other Gods before me…" Exodus 20:3.)

Chapter 4 Description:
"Before the Storm and Before the Favor of God"
(4 signifies God's work—the Creator or creation)

Chapter 5 description:
"The Favor of God"
(Of course #5 symbolizes harmony and Balance—God's favor or divine grace)

Chapter 6 description:
"Parents...Spiritual Parents are Our Heavenly Angels"
(Although #6 symbolizes imperfections, all things work together for good for those who love the Lord)

Chapter 7 description:
"Don't Get Stuck in traffic"
(We all know—or most do—that the number 7 symbolizes completion; the world was completed on the 7th day. It is done and it is good.)

Chapter 8 description:
"Don't Worry about the Haters!"
(Because the #8 means wealth and abundance. You better get yours I'm gonna get mine Glory be to God...lol)

Chapter 9 description:
:o)... Smile
(#9 means new beginnings... Isn't it good to know, after all the highs and lows of life, that God says my best is yet to come?Thank you, Daddy!)

Acknowledgments

Wow. Today is June 15, 2017 at 6:50 p.m. It has been more than five years, and now that I have my computer back its time to complete it…my baby…my novel (catch the revelation and favor!).

My dedication is to my sister Wanda Jean (Lankford) Brewer who reminded me five years ago to finish what God put in my spirit. I started my novel "2 Blessed 2 Be Stressed "on my old computer, and there was a flood in my two-story townhome, and five years later I am finishing my first story; but more is yet to come. I have a lot to say. Do you want to hear it? (We shall see…)

To my beautiful angel, my daughter Ma'Resia Rena Crump, who has always been a source of my strength, encouragement, and joy. She is my best friend, and I am so proud of her. I think she is proud of me too.

To my wonderful mama Oletha Marie Lankford, my living guardian angel and the best mom in the world. She is such a joy and blessing in my life. Thanks for all your support and encouragement always.

To my wonderful siblings and family, words can't express what your love and support have meant to me daily. I wouldn't trade you for anything in the world. I can't forget my cousin, who is like a daughter to me—Alesha and her daughter, Baby Honesty.

To all my frats/sorors and friends, your relationships have brought me so much joy and great memories. Thanks for your support also. A special thanks to my buddy Chuckie for putting the idea in my head years ago, during our Wiley College days, that I should be a writer. Also, my other sister, Ericka: we have remained in each other's lives a long time, and her friendship has been a source of encouragement.

Also, to my previous pastor and the church family. I appreciate past support through the years. I learned a lot and grew stronger after many life experiences.

**On June 17, 2017. It is finished. Thank You, Lord at 4:32 a.m. (writer hours, I guess).

Chapter 1

HATERS CAN'T DO ANYTHING FOR ME, BECAUSE (like the song says), "God favored me by Hezekiah Walker..." When you know who you are, you don't sweat the small stuff. The example God gave to me is, "Sometimes the people in your life who mean you no good, you have to treat them like an annoying fly: you either swat them away and get them out of your face, or you just keep letting them bug you." It's your choice.

Or sometimes, like when you are driving in your car, you let your window down and let them out and you keep on to your destination. It's just that simple... Again the choice is yours. What are you going to do?

God reminded me of this when I used to put too much concern and emphasis on other people. Thank You, Lord. I got delivered from people. Amen. My Lord—I like to call Him "Daddy"—said, "If you are good and pleasing in My sight, why are you worried about what he said or she said?" In other words, I like to say that people don't have a heaven or hell to put me in. Praise the Lord. Can I get an amen?

"I do believe your storm is over," like the song says. Don't ask God, "How strong do You think I am?" I am living proof that He will show you with life's challenges. I learned this the hard way.

In those times, we just have to let go and let God have His way. He will do it every time. I love to say and say often, "Too blessed to be stressed," hence the title of this book. And I don't have time to be worried about nobody's mess. (Wow. Five years later, all this blessed me, so now it's time to finish the small stuff.)

Chapter 2

PEACE, BE STILL. AND TALKING ABOUT AGREEMENT—wow. As my previous apostle always said, "Make sure what you say, you can back it up with Scripture." So, it says in Mark 4:39: "And he arose, and rebuked the wind, and said unto the sea, Peace, be still. And the wind ceased, and there was a great calm."

This is a powerful Scripture, and every time I think of it and hear this message, they share that Jesus was teaching the multitudes seaside. He discussed sowing the stony, thorny, and good ground. It was discussed why Jesus taught in parables, fruit, and harvest time. What type of seeds are you planting? (Also, Mark 4:20 -26) Mustard seeds (catch this revelation) But, when the night came, a great storm arose, and the heavy waves frightened everyone on the ship. How many times in your life have you felt frightened from the latest of "life's storms"? I know I'm not the only one who is. Yes, I have been tried and tested. Sure, I have faith in my Daddy, but still sometimes I am like, "How much longer will You allow this storm to rage in my life when I know You can make the waves cease suddenly?" This Chapter in Mark and scripture references reminds me during the low points in life while in a storm or test God gave us parables to apply to our daily lives. There are three parables listed the sower, the seed growing, the mustard seed and verse 35 Jesus calms the storm. (I am blessing myself right now.)

Alright, let me get back to the emphasis on this chapter. This passage Mark 4:35-41 is a friendly reminder—Jesus's testimony was, "Look, didn't I cause the storm to cease, the waves to stop raging, and didn't I give you the peace I promised you? And, if I did it back then, hallelujah, I can do it again. So, don't you dare doubt me 'oh ye of little faith.'" I often say, "Lord…yes Daddy, I know and I believe, but please help my unbelief."

So, this is to encourage myself and others to not fret or get discouraged. Yes, the storms of life will come, but you can and will get past this journey in life if you have the right agreement. Your relationship, my relationship, a real relationship with God is the peace you need to surpass all understanding (Phil. 4:7).

This is enough to rejoice and shout about right now. Amen! It may be a little cloudy in my life right now, but I can see the sun shining, and better days are ahead. I declare and receive it in Jesus's name.

Chapter 3

ONE OF MY FAVORITE SONGS IS "WELL DONE" BY Deitrick Haddon. The song and the video often remind me of what will I say on that great day-the day I meet my Lord and savior. I don't mean to be morbid or over-emotional, but I have a vivid image of that moment. It brings a sense of joy, happiness, and relief that I made it. I wonder, will I have any words? Will I just cry and fall at His feet and say, "Daddy"? I am trying not to cry right at this moment. The song ends saying, "You can come on in." (love this song "Well Done" by Deitrick Haddon)

I love my daughter, my family, and my life. I can't complain. But many times, during rough moments in my life, it brings me comfort to know there is a greater purpose for it all. This brings me a great source of joy and encouragement. Yes, I do want to see my loved ones again in heaven. I have been blessed to live with this sense of being Daddy's girl or God's baby girl, and what child doesn't love their daddy or to be in his presence? I was so fortunate to have an awesome and amazing daddy—Lee Elute Lankford. He was the patriarch of our family, which means heritage. The definition of patriarch for anyone who may want to know is the male head of a family or tribe, or any of those biblical figures regarded of the human race, elder or leader. I was watching a family tv series with Sally Field called *Brothers & Sisters* (loved this show and my siblings); they referred to their father by this title, and it stuck with me. Heritage referenced in vocabulary.com can also refer to a person's ethnic or cultural background. I'm so grateful my family and heritage included two loving parents with seven siblings who always loved God and each other…we are blessed…Our family has grown over the years as the youngest girl I'm excited to pass down my wisdom to the young in our family.

So, this chapter is a summation from me; it is my words, my song, and my testimony. So, my life hasn't always been perfect, and neither have I, but my desire is always to do my Father's will and to hear Him say one day, "Well done, my faithful child. You got discouraged, frightened, and irritated; you were happy, and you were sad; you loved, and you lost, but you never quit; and for that, I am so proud of you my baby girl!" (My heart and spirit are smiling right now.)

I love you. –Father, Son, and the Holy Ghost

"Thou shalt have no other gods before me" (Exodus 20:3). You alone are worthy of all my praise.

Chapter 4

BEFORE ANY STORM, IT GETS DARK; THEN THE RAINS, thunder, and lightning start. Life is a cycle. We have warnings before each tragedy in our lives. Sometimes, we are too busy to hear or discern what God is trying to tell us in our spirits. ("Help us, Lord," like I often say.) The good news is that during dark or lonely times in life, God says in Deuteronomy 31:6, "Be strong and courageous. Do not be afraid or terrified because of them, for the Lord your God goes with you; he will never leave you nor forsake you." Psalm 46:5 (GWT) says, "God is in that city. It cannot fail. God will help it at the break of dawn." The storms in life may come, but they will not last.

I like to say, "If you survived the hurricanes, tornados, tsunamis, floods, typhoons, and other natural disasters of this life, you can survive a little rain." The moral of the story is that when you have gone through the lowest points in your life, now is time to reap your harvest. It's time to receive the favor of God for your faithfulness, service, and stewardship, because our Father wants our lives to be about more than just surviving storms and barely living. Favor means approval, support, or liking someone or something; an act of kindness beyond what is due or usual. I am so ready to live in the favor of God. Anybody with me?

Let Your glory shine bright in my life right now, Lord. I declare and decree it shall be so, and it begins with me.

Hallelujah!

God is our creator, and in this season of life, we cannot fail to hear His voice. He will direct our steps to the next phase in our lives. Are you ready? Don't miss it.

It's my time and my season to be blessed. I receive it in Jesus's name! Amen.

Chapter 5

ARE YOU TRULY READY FOR THE FAVOR OF GOD IN your life? There is a quote I may have heard in a song or read online that says, "When God grants you His favor, nothing can stop the blessings he has in store for you." Another, I read on google or facebook recently is, "Other people may have more talent, education, or experience but God's favor can cause you to go to places you could not go on your own." Proverbs 8:35 says, "For he who finds me finds life and obtains favor from the Lord."

Another Scripture I am very fond of is Jeremiah 29:11, which says, "For I know the thoughts that I have towards you, saith the Lord, thoughts of peace, and not of evil, to give you an expected end."

It's ok to remember this Scripture or have several talks with the Lord when your life isn't going exactly the way you planned. I often have talks with my beautiful baby girl and say, "Angel (that's what I call her), life is full of choices—good and bad— and lessons we learn, but don't ever regret any of it. We learn from it all: the heartbreaks, the disappointments, happiness, and the joys. When we start to second guess ourselves or doubt why did I do this or that, it is all just precious time we can't get back."

I promise you we learned something, whether it was great and we loved that memory or moment, or that situation didn't work out the way I had anticipated. In those cases, wisdom says next time I will handle it differently. The point that I am trying to make is that life is what we make it. I choose joy and happiness. I want only the best for my daughter, my family, church family, ministries, friends, etc.

We can have what we speak, declare, or decree. Declaring and decreeing, "It's my time to reap my harvest. I been sowing a long time and have been through a lot, but my Daddy says I don't look like what I have been through because His favor has been on me.'"

One of my favorite Scriptures (one that me and Darnell aka my Darniepooh/my nephew who is also like a son to me quote all the time) is Isaiah 54:17 (NKJV), "No weapons formed against you shall prosper, and every tongue which rises against you in judgement You shall condemn This is the heritage of the servants of the Lord, and their righteousness is from Me, says the Lord."

Chapter 5

Catch this revelation. What God has for you is for you—harmony, balance, and God's divine favor and grace.

Amen.

Chapter 6

WHAT DO PARENTS HAVE IN COMMON WITH HEAVenly angels? Whether they are natural, spiritual, or biological parents, their primary duty is to provide for their children. They protect them from danger, and they bless them with words and wisdom all the days of their lives. They provide food, shelter, and love. They are the sole sense of goodness about themselves, their lives, and their future. They are and always will be their children's everything, while on this earth and even when they leave us. Our nation is struggling with our family unit. I was fortunate to have both my parents for all of my adult life. For a lot of people who I know don't have these strong family bonds or connections, it really makes a difference in giving one a strong, solid foundation from childhood to your adult life.

I am rich and blessed beyond measure for this little simple fact. I didn't realize how special and significant this was. I have tried to provide this for my family, even though I wasn't able to keep my family together for my child at an early age. She has had to experience divorce and family separation, not once but twice. I still look at her and only see my beautiful baby girl, my angel, and my friend. She is such a blessing to me. She has a good relationship with her dad and our family. She continually makes her mama so proud just with a smile. She has always been wise beyond her years (maybe she will write her book sometime; she truly has a story, and she can cover psychology, too, as this is her major and course of study).

I am so grateful for all that I have learned from my beautiful living guarding angel, Oletha Marie Lankford. Words can't express how her hugs, her wake up calls, and her prayers have enriched my life. I am truly blessed and triumphant to say I am her "baby girl." She always says we learn something daily. She has been such a great Godly example of what a woman should be. A Proverbs 31 mom. I always joke and say, "Mama, if I am half the woman that you are, then I will be almost as awesome as you."

This weekend is Father's Day, and my daddy has been gone almost nine years, but he is always in our hearts and spirits. June is sometimes bittersweet for me; there's Father's Day, he passed on June 19th, his funeral on the twenty-eighth, and his birthday on thirtieth. However, I treasure the wonderful memories we had and smile when I see him in my awesome brothers, nephews, and uncle (I only have one left, his only living brother—Uncle Iziar). Also, I see the display of fatherhood in my ex-husbands, frats, Wileyites, and great friends. I can't forget my past apostle. I see such wonderful examples of amazing fathers and role models. I love and admire their relationships with their babies. How could I be sad with all that love around? Right? The world needs more of this exemplary strength and bond.

In summation, I can't forget about all spiritual leaders that have poured into my life also. They have empowered and encouraged me. They pushed me to never quit or give up, and to strive daily to be all that God has called me to be. These never-ending priceless lessons can never be ignored or forgotten.

"All things work together for good to those who love God, to those who are called according to his purpose" (Rom. 8:28 NKJV). I am not perfect, but God is not through working on me. Praise the Lord!

Chapter 7

OKAY, DON'T GET STUCK IN TRAFFIC. WHEN GOD gave me the revelation for this chapter five years ago, I was traveling to work and, as usual, got stuck in traffic. But there was a greater point that was revealed to me. As I began to talk, vent, or fuss with God during my usual daily commute, I said, "Oh, Lord, oh no. Not right now. I am running late." So, I prayed that everyone was okay and repeated, "Lord, split this traffic like the Red Sea." What I didn't realize was that the accident had already happened, and it was actually on the side of the road, and the wait wasn't really that long.

Moral of the story: don't get frustrated when we get stuck in life, or when there are emotional delays or obstacles in our way. Yes, we may not be able to see which way to go, but the good news is that we don't need to. When we pray, trust, and believe our heavenly Father who sees everything, He will always make a way and provide and protect us through the dangers of this world. Where is your faith? What has really frustrated you lately?

"Now unto him that is able to do exceedingly above all that we ask or think, according to the power that worketh in us" (Eph. 3:20).

Also, sometimes we just have to slow down and spend quality time with God. He is trying to protect us from the dangers ahead—the road blocks, potholes, and construction. In our busy lives, we can't keep running past our heavenly Father; that is when the problems occur. "Slow down baby," or "Take your time, boo," like my little brother says all the time.

This chapter symbolizes completion. "Being confident of this very thing, that he which hath begun a good work in you will perform it until the day of Jesus Christ" (Phil. 1:6 KJV).

"And God saw everything that he had made, and behold, it was very good. And the evening and morning were the sixth day" (Gen. 1:31).

"Thus the heavens and the earth were finished, and all the host of them" (Gen. 2:1 KJV).

Chapter 8

DON'T WORRY ABOUT YOUR HATERS. THEY ARE gonna be there, and it doesn't matter what you do or don't do. The saying goes that you can't please everyone all the time. This life has taught and reminded me that there is only one perfect person in this world. His name was Jesus Christ, and guess what? They still crucified Him. He died for our sins; the same people who praised Him one moment, betrayed him with a kiss and laughed as He was beaten up the hill on Calvary the next. So why you are tripping because that person ignored you? Didn't appreciate you? Didn't value you? Didn't realize your worth? Didn't see your heart and inner beauty? Trust me, this was a hard pill for me to swallow also. I am still learning that it is a gift to be a person of integrity and loyalty. It is a gift, do you hear me? You will be disappointed a lot in life when you expect it from everyone.

If you are reading this and you are like me (a person with a big heart), you be encouraged right now; beloved, this chapter is for us. It's okay to be that way, for love is the greatest gift. "And now abides faith, hope, love, these three; but the greatest of these is love." So, unfortunately, this is a spiritual gift and the greatest, so we love harder and deeper. Sometimes the hurt is also greater, but Lord have mercy—it is worth it, but there is a cost. My Lord. I am feeling this Scripture right now.

Alright, the number eight symbolizes in the Bible a new beginning, meaning a new order or creation. I am excited because I am ready for my new beginning. I am declaring my season of lack is over; it is time for wealth and abundance, not just for me but for all my family, natural and spiritual. I don't know about you, but I have struggled, had my good days and bad days. I am ready to do the next assignment in my life, which is to help others. This takes resources. So, I am grateful for what I know God is about to do. I speak it and am then ready to receive more to be a blessing to someone else. It's time; God is ready to do it suddenly. I say, "Do it, Daddy." I pray. Trust and believe now, I am awaiting your manifestation in my life. Amen.

Chapter 9
Smile

WOW, IT IS GREAT TO KNOW THAT AFTER ALL YOU have been through in life, you can smile because it's only going to get better. Kirk Franklin has a song called "I Smile." He started off with some dedications, and it says, "Today's a new day." How many times do we wake up in the morning asking God, why this or that? When we wake, we should have our prayer, conversation, or praise time with God; we should smile knowing He's working it out in our lives, in our favor. Whatever season you are in life, whatever chapter you may be in—happiness, loneliness, sadness, or excitement about the future—look back and realize it is all working together for your good. I hope my First book made you laugh, maybe cry and hopefully smile. But, while you look in the mirror, don't forget to smile. You look so much better when you smile. I was told once, during my college days at Wiley College, "You always smile like you never have any problems." I look serious a lot of times now and often quiet.

This chapter is a reminder for me to always have a joy and peace that this world can't take from me. I heard Shirley Caesar singing "This joy that I have the world didn't give it to me and if the world didn't give it the world can't take it away." Amen.

Praise for nine symbolizes birthing out something new. It is encouragement to me that God is not through with us yet. All things are working out according to His plan, not ours. There is a blessing in the lesson. I am excited for what God is doing in my life right now.

I pray I was obedient and finished my short book of encouragement and wisdom. "Too blessed to be stressed!" is something I often say and mean. I hope that it gives you strength and guidance, and, if nothing else, know that you are not alone. Someone hears and feels ya and is excited for your future and spiritual growth.

Sincerely from me to you,

Lesia R. Lankford

www.ingramcontent.com/pod-product-compliance
Ingram Content Group UK Ltd.
Pitfield, Milton Keynes, MK11 3LW, UK
UKHW022218230426
12048UKWH00016BA/912